Hope for
Hard Times

Hope for Hard Times

Scott Hahn

Our Sunday Visitor Publishing Division
Our Sunday Visitor, Inc.
Huntington, Indiana 46750

Nihil Obstat: Msgr. Michael Heintz, Ph.D.
Censor Librorum

Imprimatur: ✠ John M. D'Arcy
Bishop of Fort Wayne-South Bend
November 14, 2009

Contents

Let nothing disturb you; Let nothing frighten you. All things are passing. God never changes. Patience obtains all things. Nothing is wanting to him who possesses God. God alone suffices.

— BOOKMARK FOUND IN
ST. TERESA OF ÁVILA'S BREVIARY

CHAPTER 1

Is This How You Treat Your Friends?

The only tragedy in life is not to be a saint.

— Léon Bloy

All St. Teresa of Ávila wanted to do was to live a life of simple poverty and prayer. But living a godly life seems like a deliberate insult to a world in love with worldliness, and she had more than her share of hard times. She was denounced to the Inquisition. She was treated with contempt and cruelty by wealthy would-be patrons who wanted her to run her convents their way. Instead of quiet contemplation, she suffered through a life filled with confrontation and opposition.

Well, one day, she had had enough, and she let loose a torrent of complaint to Our Lord.

"But, Teresa," God replied, "this is how I treat *all* my friends."

"Well," the saint answered, "no wonder you have so few!"

Teresa's complaint could have arisen, just as credibly, from any of the friends of God we encounter in the Bible. Think of Abel, at the dawn of history, as he lay dying and vanquished by his wicked brother. Think of Noah, suffering through the dull monotony of a month of rain, living in close quarters with animals while his world washed away. Think of Abraham, the only person whom the Bible *names* as a "friend of God" (Jas 2:23): he endured many ordeals, culminating in the call to sacrifice his only son!

The patriarch Joseph, too, was favored by God — but was sold into slavery, falsely accused of adultery, and imprisoned. Moses, David, and Jeremiah knew their own calamities. Then there's Job, who lost his home, family, and health — and he *hadn't done anything wrong.* It wasn't a punishment he deserved. It just happened.

Finally, consider the Virgin Mary. She believed what God promised her at the Annunciation. Yet she also knew there was a dark side to the promise. Simeon the priest had prophesied that she would know great sorrow:

> "Behold, this child is set for the fall and rising of many in Israel, and for a sign that is spoken against . . . and a sword will pierce through your own soul also."

— Lk 2:34-35

Thirty-some years later, she knew what he meant. There at the foot of the Cross, she saw her Son crucified as the worst of criminals — a traitor, a terrorist.

Is this the way God treats his friends?

If so, do we really want to be God's friends?

Well, yes and yes. We recognize a certain pattern in the lives of those who are faithful to God. They undergo trials and suffering. Yet they always emerge as the most enviable people on earth.

They are enviable because they live in hope for the possession of something we all desire: love.

Only Love Satisfies

Love is the only thing that fulfills us, and so we all hunger for it. Love, however, always requires sacrifice.

True love always requires sacrifice.

This is true even of human loves. We give up the "freedom" of living alone for the greater freedom of marriage to our beloved. We part with a large chunk of our savings account in order to buy an engagement ring. We gladly forego pleasures that would require us to be away from our loved ones.

The literature of romance is replete with stories of vigils, journeys, ordeals, and outlandish gifts.

Why? Because love is something worth suffering for — even earthly love, though every earthly love is finite.

The *Catechism of the Catholic Church* teaches us, "Love causes a desire for the absent good and the hope of obtaining it" (1765). St. Thomas Aquinas clarifies that the absent good, in the case of love, is an arduous good, a difficult good.

> *Suffering is a great favor. Remember that every-thing soon comes to an end . . . and take courage. Think of how our gain is eternal.*
> — St. Teresa of Ávila

People endure difficulties for love's sake every day.

How much, then, can we endure for true love, eternal love, the love that satisfies — divine love? If you and I awaited something so great as the love promised to Abraham and the Blessed Virgin and Teresa of Ávila, what could we endure for it? Pain? Suffering? Abandonment? Misunderstanding? To be victimized by evil?

Hope could carry us through all those things, as it carries all God's friends.

They can endure and persevere because love is stronger than any torment they must face.

Times may be hard, yes, but hope is more durable. It's one of only three things that abide (see 1 Cor 13:13).

Take Away

Saints and Scriptures teach us that hardship need not make us unhappy.

CHAPTER 2

What Are We Waiting For?

To those who seek the kingdom of God and his righteousness, he has promised to give all else besides. Since everything indeed belongs to God, he who possesses God wants for nothing, if he himself is not found wanting before God.

— St. Cyprian of Carthage

How do we have hope, though, when we're miserable? Not just miserable like having a fever and body aches, but *miserable* — like having our homes destroyed and being carried off to exile in Babylon?

At the root of all misery is unfulfilled desire.

We want economic prosperity — or even just stability. We want relief from bodily pain. We want family members to get along for a change. We want our coworkers and neighbors to treat us with respect. We want to raise children to be moral and happy adults.

These are important things, no doubt. But are they reasonable objects of our hope?

Scripture certainly leads us to believe they are. In the Bible, we find men and women praying for all manner of earthly goods, and having God answer their prayers, seemingly on their terms.

Why, then, must *we* suffer through hard times, in spite of all the prayers we've raised for relief?

The answer, perhaps, is in the object of our hope. Are we hoping, ultimately, for earthly happiness — or are we hoping in God?

True hope seeks only the Kingdom of God, and is convinced that all earthly things necessary for this life will without doubt be given. . . . The heart cannot have peace until it acquires this hope.

— St. Seraphim of Sarov

Just a few years ago, many Americans began to pray the biblical prayer of Jabez so that they might increase their earthly wealth. However, I noticed no corresponding surge in the number of millionaires in the city where I live. Atheists will laugh and say there was no god to answer those prayers. A Catholic, however, would be right to say that God sometimes says yes to such prayers, but often says no, according to the greater need of the person who asks.

The greater need is not financial. It's spiritual. It's the need for a love that satisfies. And that is always a reasonable object of our hope.

God sometimes gives us what we want — even money — so that we'll learn to trust him to give us what we need.

When he "answers" prayers in earthly terms, those are not final answers, as the earthly objects cannot satisfy us for long. The earthly gifts do not bring happiness the way love does, and that is a lesson we can learn by looking around us. There is no shortage of miserable millionaires, miserable people who have perfect bodily health, miserable people who have steady, well-paying jobs.

God sometimes gives us what we want so that we'll learn to trust him to give us what we need.

Sometimes, we need to learn those lessons by personal experience of misery amid earthly success. Sometimes, we learn our lessons by personal experience of failing to achieve our modest earthly goals, in spite of our ardent prayers.

God can answer all prayers because he is the all-powerful creator. He answers them the way he does because he is our Father.

Take Away

Our greatest need is for a love that satisfies. Only God's love satisfies.

CHAPTER 3

How Our Father Loves

"Give us": The trust of children who look to their Father for everything is beautiful . . . Jesus teaches us this petition, because it glorifies our Father by acknowledging how good he is, beyond all goodness.
— CATECHISM OF THE CATHOLIC CHURCH, 2828

Remember how you hated being punished when you were little? Maybe you thought your parents hated you. It wasn't *your* fault you broke the rules. Or maybe yes, it was, but that's no reason you should be *punished* for it.

Now that we're older, we understand how difficult it is to discipline children. Some of us have children of our own, and when they break the rules, we know we can't just let them get away with it.

Yet we know that punishment hurts them, and we hate hurting them. That's how it is with children: sometimes what you know is good for them isn't what *feels* good to them — or to you.

We know that, but it's still easy to forget it when we're children. The letter to the Hebrews reminds us that we're *God's* children.

Heb 12:5-6

5 And have you forgotten the exhortation
    which addresses you as sons? —
"My son, do not regard lightly the discipline
    of the Lord, nor lose courage when
      you are punished by him.
6 For the Lord disciplines him whom he loves,
    and chastises every son whom he receives."

What does it really mean that we're God's children? It means that he really loves us, enough to treat us the way a good father treats his children. He loves us enough to discipline us.

Heb 12:7-11

7 It is for discipline that you have to endure. God is treating you as sons; for what son is there whom his father does not discipline? 8 If you are left without discipline, in which all have participated, then you are illegitimate children and not sons. 9 Besides this, we have

had earthly fathers to discipline us and we respected them. Shall we not much more be subject to the Father of spirits and live? [10] For they disciplined us for a short time at their pleasure, but he disciplines us for our good, that we may share his holiness. [11] For the moment all discipline seems painful rather than pleasant; later it yields the peaceful fruit of righteousness to those who have been trained by it.

There's something shocking, but also consoling, in what Hebrews tells us about discipline. We all suffer through hard times, but Hebrews tells us that the hard times aren't signs of God's anger. Instead, they're signs of God's love.

If we didn't have the hard times, we wouldn't know God loved us.

If we didn't have the hard times, we wouldn't know God loved us.

How many times did our parents tell us exactly the same thing about discipline? "I do it because I love you."

Yeah, right, we said to ourselves when we were eight years old. *You do it because you hate me and like making me miserable.*

But now that we've grown up, we tell our own children the very same thing; what's more, we know how true it is with every fiber of our being.

Punished by Pleasing

If we hated our children — if we just wanted to get rid of them — then we'd let them do whatever they wanted. We certainly wouldn't spend hours trying to make them do their homework or sort out their messes. We'd just give them total freedom without consequences. Pretty soon, they'd fall off the roof or be run over by a train, and we'd be free to do whatever we wanted without worrying about what the kids were up to.

But we love them, so we discipline them. We make sure they know there are consequences for getting in trouble, so that they won't suffer the much worse consequences of being left completely on their own.

That's why Hebrews tells us that the hard times are how we know God is our Father. If he just left us skipping merrily down the pathway to destruction, we wouldn't be his children at all. We'd be "illegitimate," to use the striking term we find in Hebrews.

But we're God's *real* children, which means that God loves us enough to discipline us. And it's unpleasant — as unpleasant as it was when we were eight years old and got sent to our rooms on a summer afternoon. (And if you don't think that compares in unpleasantness to the hard times adults have to go through, then you should ask an eight-year-old.)

> I would like to make everyone understand the great grace that God, in his mercy, bestows when He sends suffering . . . Then indeed the soul is purified like gold in the furnace; without knowing it, it becomes radiant and is set free to take flight to its Good.
> — St. Paul of the Cross

Discipline isn't the same as wrath: discipline is a father punishing his kids because he can't stop loving them. When we read about the awful things that happened to Israel and Judah, or when we think about the equally awful things happening in the world today, we think of God's "wrath" — but we should really think of God's love.

That's the hardest part of our faith to learn, just as it was hard for us to believe that our own parents were disciplining us because they loved us.

But God has ways of helping us learn. As usual, we may not like them — but we'll thank him for them in the end.

His discipline itself is a reason for our hope. It is proof that he loves us as a father loves his children. Faith enables us to accept what our Father tells us, because we accept his authority. Hope enables to trust that his word is reliable and his care is abiding. We can hope because we have faith.

Take Away

God's discipline is proof of his fatherly love.

CHAPTER 4

Testing Our Faith

*Abraham was firmly convinced
that he who said to him,
"through Isaac shall your descendants be named,"
was not lying.*

— St. Ephrem the Syrian

We already mentioned the story of how Abraham was told to sacrifice Isaac, his only son — and how Abraham was willing to do it. It was a test of his faith, the book of Genesis tells us. And it was a test of his hope, a test he would pass. St. Paul reflected on Abraham: "In hope he believed against hope, that he should become the father of many nations" (Rom 4:18) — and this would happen in spite of his childlessness, in spite of his advanced age, in spite of all the facts in the world.

Isaac was an impossibility, a miracle, to begin with. He was Abraham's most impossible dream come true. That was what God was asking him to give up. Every child is a special miracle, but this wasn't just every child. Isaac was the impossible and miraculous fulfillment of all God's promises to Abraham.

Yet Abraham had faith in God. He might not understand it, he might not like it, but he knew that God's way was the right way.

Gen 22:3-6

³ So Abraham rose early in the morning, saddled his donkey and took two of his young men with him, and his son Isaac; and he cut the wood for the burnt offering, and arose and went to the place of which God had told him. ⁴ On the third day Abraham lifted up his eyes and saw the place afar off.

⁵ Then Abraham said to his young men, "Stay here with the donkey; I and the lad will go yonder and worship, and come again to you."

⁶ And Abraham took the wood of the burnt offering, and laid it on Isaac his son; and he took in his hand the fire and the knife. So they went both of them together.

Notice, by the way, that Isaac is carrying the wood for his own sacrifice. He's not a little boy anymore: by this time, he's a strong young man. We tend to forget it, but ancient Jewish teachers and the early Christian writers were very much aware of it: the sacrifice of Isaac was not simply a matter of Abraham tying up his son against his will. Isaac, the strong young man, participated completely and willingly: if he had tried to get away, he could certainly have overpowered his ancient father.

Gen 22:7-8

[7] And Isaac said to his father Abraham,
    "My father!"
And he said, "Here am I, my son."
He said, "Behold, the fire and the wood; but
    where is the lamb for a burnt offering?"
[8] Abraham said, "God will provide himself
    the lamb for a burnt offering, my son."
So they went both of them together.

We have to pause here and admire how the master craftsman who gave us this story simultaneously builds up the suspense and paints Abraham's emotional state with a quick stroke. Isaac is working on putting two and two together: he knows that they're going to make a sacrifice, but he doesn't see the animal. He may well be starting to suspect the truth. But if he does, he still has faith in God and in his father Abraham.

Gen 22:9-14

[9] When they came to the place of which God had told him, Abraham built an altar there, and laid the wood in order, and bound Isaac his son, and laid him on the altar, upon the wood. [10] Then Abraham put forth his hand, and took the knife to slay his son.

[11] But the angel of the LORD called to him from heaven, and said, "Abraham, Abraham!" And he said, "Here am I."

[12] He said, "Do not lay your hand on the lad or do anything to him; for now I know that you fear God, seeing you have not withheld your son, your only son, from me."

[13] And Abraham lifted up his eyes and looked, and behold, behind him was a ram, caught in a thicket by his horns; and Abraham went and took the ram, and offered it up as a burnt offering instead of his son. [14] So Abraham called the name of that place The LORD will provide; as it is said to this day, "On the mount of the LORD it shall be provided."

So our story has a happy ending. For all God's faithful people, the story always has a happy ending. We just don't necessarily get it on *this* side of the grave, the way Abraham did.

It would be easy to say that our faith will never be tested like Abraham's. It would be easy, and it would be wrong.

Loss Is Inevitable

The fact is that every one of us will be called on to give up what we simply can't imagine giving up.

> *Every one of us will be called on to give up what we simply can't imagine giving up.*

A mother, a father, a wife, a husband, a child — who among us would willingly give up any one of those?

Yet God will demand it of us, just as he did of Abraham. Sooner or later, we're going to have to give up some of the people we love most. At the end of earthly life, we will have to part ways with all of them.

Why? Not because God is cruel or capricious, but because it's necessary — both for the ones we love and for ourselves.

We know that heaven is our destination — at least we know it with our brains. Our hearts don't always keep up with our brains. But we have to have

Abraham's faith, a faith in nothing less than the resurrection.

Heb 11:17-19

[17] By faith Abraham, when he was tested, offered up Isaac, and he who had received the promises was ready to offer up his only son, [18] of whom it was said, "Through Isaac shall your descendants be named." [19] He considered that God was able to raise men even from the dead; hence, figuratively speaking, he did receive him back.

God had promised Abraham that Isaac would carry on his family; now God was seemingly contradicting himself. It's true that God doesn't make promises he won't keep . . . but he does make promises that won't come true on this side of the grave.

God tests our faith just the way he did Abraham's.

Now, when we hear that "God tested Abraham," we probably start to imagine God as some sort of grade-school teacher. One of the mean teachers, the kind who would suddenly announce a pop quiz just because he was sure you hadn't been paying attention.

That isn't the kind of test God gives us.

One of the perks that go with omniscience is knowing the heart of every human being already. God knows what faith we have: he doesn't need to devise elaborate experiments to find out.

Don't wince under the hammer that strikes you. Have an eye to the chisel that cuts you and to the hand that shapes you. The skillful and loving Architect may wish to make you one of the chief stones of his eternal edifice and the fairest statues in his kingdom. Then let him do it. He loves you. He knows what he is doing. He has had experience. All his blows are skillful and straight and loving. He never misses, unless you cause him to by your impatience.

— St. Louis de Montfort

But we don't know our own faith. When human teachers administer tests, they want to find out what we know. God knows all, but tests us so that we can find out things we didn't know about ourselves. The tests confront us with our own weakness, and give us a greater awareness of how much more we need God's strength.

That's why even the bad times are good things.

In fact, we might say that *especially* the bad times are good things.

Discipline Is Not Punishment

The fact is that God doesn't punish us with bad times: he *disciplines* us with bad times. There's a big difference.

The way God *punishes* people is by letting them have everything they want (see Rom 1:18-28). If you see someone who seems to be prospering in wickedness, that's probably someone who's turned away from God so completely that nothing will bring him back. Nothing is left for him but to follow that broad, pleasant road that leads straight to hell (see Mt 7:13).

So there's your answer to why the wicked often prosper while the virtuous suffer: it's because God loves the virtuous enough to discipline them, knowing that the discipline can bring them back to him when they stray.

The discipline may seem harsh — but that's our human point of view intruding. As Christians, we have to get used to seeing things from a long-term point of view — a Christian point of view.

If God allows you to suffer much, it's a sign that he has great designs for you and that he certainly intends to make you a saint.

— St. Ignatius Loyola

If we really believe what we say we believe, then the life we live on earth is only a small part of the whole story. No matter how painful what happens to us here is, we need to keep heaven in view. If we do that, we'll realize that our worst nightmares are just temporary inconveniences. Even death — even the worst kind of death — is not the end of the story. The things we fear most stand between us and heaven, but we know that we can endure them and come out the other side.

But that doesn't stop them from hurting. It doesn't keep hard times from being hard. And here's a little secret you might not have learned in CCD class: when the times get hard, sometimes even the saints complain.

Take Away

All love requires sacrifice.

CHAPTER 5

Complaining to God

He served his master, though with complaint.
He wasn't a plaster sort of saint.
— PHYLLIS McGINLEY, ON ST. JEROME

The biggest book of the Bible is the book of Psalms, the prayer book of the people of God. It's filled with hymns for every occasion — for liturgies, for private devotions, for all the joys and sorrows that human life is filled with.

And as long as we're quoting statistics, here's another statistic that most of us don't think about: More than forty percent of the Psalms are songs of "complaint" or lament. That's getting up pretty close to half.

That surprises us. More than that, it dumbfounds us. Who would dare to complain to God?

Actually, complaining to God is one of the privileges of being God's children. But we have to understand the difference between *complaining* and *grumbling*.

Grumbling is what the Israelites did in the wilderness. They complained *about* God, not *to* God. In fact, they were ready to fire him and get themselves a god they liked better — that's why they had Aaron build them a golden calf.

Complaining is not the same thing as grumbling or murmuring.

The consequences of grumbling could be severe. St. Paul reminded his Corinthian friends of what happened to the rebellious Israelites in the desert:

> We must not put the Lord to the test, as some of them did and were destroyed by serpents; nor grumble, as some of them did and were destroyed by the Destroyer. Now these things happened to them as a warning, but they were written down for our instruction, upon whom the end of the ages has come.
>
> — 1 COR 10:9-11

Psalm-Sung Blues

So grumbling — complaining about God — is bad. But complaining *to* God is different. If you complain to someone, you assume that it's someone who really cares about you.

Ps 102:3-4

³ For my days pass away like smoke,
and my bones burn like a furnace.
⁴ My heart is smitten like grass, and
withered;
I forget to eat my bread.

The poet, identified only as "one afflicted," complains to God about his affliction. But he complains, not because he thinks God is doing a lousy job of running the universe, but because he believes that God can do something about his troubles. And, because of this belief, he holds on to a reasonable hope:

Ps 102:16-17

¹⁶ For the LORD will build up Zion,
he will appear in his glory;
¹⁷ he will regard the prayer of the destitute,
and will not despise their supplication.

This faith is obvious even in the gloomiest of the Psalms. By far the best-known Psalm of complaint is Psalm 22, the one Christ himself quoted just before he died on the cross:

Ps 22

[1] My God, my God, why have you
    forsaken me?
Why are you so far from helping me, from
    the words of my groaning?
[2] O my God, I cry by day, but you do not
    answer;
    and by night, but find no rest.

So far, it sounds gloomy enough. But David (to
whom this Psalm is attributed) doesn't get very far
before he expresses his confidence in God:

[3] Yet you are holy,
    enthroned on the praises of Israel.
[4] In you our fathers trusted;
    they trusted, and you delivered them.
[5] To you they cried, and were saved;
    in you they trusted, and were not disappointed.

That confidence doesn't make the present troubles go away, and it hardly even makes them easier
to deal with:

[6] But I am a worm, and no man;
    scorned by men, and despised by the people.
[7] All who see me mock at me,
    they make mouths at me, they wag their heads;

⁸ "He committed his cause to the LORD;
     let him deliver him,
  let him rescue him, for he delights in him!"

Still, David knows that God has kept him safe throughout his life, and all his hope is built on the faith that God will not really forsake him, in spite of all appearances.

⁹ Yet you are he who took me from the womb;
    you kept me safe upon my mother's breasts.
¹⁰ Upon you was I cast from my birth,
    and since my mother bore me
      you have been my God.

This isn't a rebel cursing the king. This is a son begging his Father for help. That's the wonderful thing about the Psalms of complaint: they give us a childlike freedom to approach God as a Father.

Playing God

"If I were a father," we say — complaining the way our own children complain to us — "If I were a father, I would never put my kids through what you're putting us through."

But notice that's not where the psalmist ends. In spite of his complaints, he goes on to express his faith in God: "I would never put my kids through what you're putting us through. But you're a better father than I could ever hope to be. You're stronger, wiser, and more loving than I am."

You can't just end with the complaint, because then you've only made yourself miserable. Complaining doesn't feel good unless you go on from there. You have to make an act of faith.

Hundreds of years before Jesus' resurrection, the psalmists knew that their complaints weren't really complete until they'd made that act of faith and hope — until they'd expressed their confidence that, however deep their troubles, however unbearable their pain, God would still come through for them in the end.

So we shouldn't be afraid to come to God with complaints in our prayers. But we shouldn't stop with the complaints. We have to remember the acts of faith and hope.

With me prayer is a lifting up of the heart, a look toward heaven, a cry of gratitude and love uttered equally in sorrow and in joy; in a word, something noble, supernatural, which enlarges my soul and unites it to God.

— St. Thérèse of Lisieux

The psalmists knew that, and we can't afford to forget it — not after God has spent thousands of years showing the world time and again how he brings the greatest good from the greatest evil. For this is exactly what happened when Jesus was crucified. The Crucifixion was the most horrific sin mankind ever committed against God. Yet it brought about the greatest good: our salvation.

But why? Why does it sometimes take great evil to bring great good? Couldn't God be nice about it and bring the greatest good out of, say, the greatest good?

As often happens, we can find the answer in St. Paul. It turns out that what we think of as "good" isn't necessarily what's really good for us at all.

Take Away

It's OK to complain to God. He can take it.

CHAPTER 6

Power Made Perfect

> *St. Augustine . . . defines prayer as an exercise of desire. Man was created for greatness — for God himself; he was created to be filled by God. But his heart is too small for the greatness to which it is destined. It must be stretched. "By delaying [his gift], God strengthens our desire; through desire he enlarges our soul and by expanding it he increases its capacity [for receiving him]."*
>
> — POPE BENEDICT XVI, *SPE SALVI* 33

Whenever we're in trouble, we should remember that Jesus taught us to pray without ceasing.

Lk 11:5-8

⁵ And he said to them, "Which of you who has a friend will go to him at midnight and say to him, 'Friend, lend me three loaves; ⁶ for a friend of mine has arrived on a journey, and I have nothing to set before him'; ⁷ and he will

answer from within, 'Do not bother me; the door is now shut, and my children are with me in bed; I cannot get up and give you anything'? [8] I tell you, though he will not get up and give him anything because he is his friend, yet because of his importunity he will rise and give him whatever he needs."

It's really a funny image. We should keep asking God, and eventually he'll give us what we need just to shut us up!

The catch here, of course, is that God gives us what we *need,* not necessarily what we *want.* In fact, what we need is sometimes exactly the opposite of what we want.

We see that even with Jesus himself, because even Jesus didn't always get what he asked for. Remember how he prayed in the Garden of Gethsemane.

Lk 22:39-46

[39] And he came out, and went, as was his custom, to the Mount of Olives; and the disciples followed him. [40] And when he came to the place he said to them, "Pray that you may not enter into temptation." [41] And he withdrew from them about a stone's throw, and knelt

down and prayed, [42] "Father, if you are willing, remove this cup from me; nevertheless not my will, but yours, be done." [43] And there appeared to him an angel from heaven, strengthening him. [44] And being in agony he prayed more earnestly; and his sweat became like great drops of blood falling down on the ground.

[45] And when he rose from prayer, he came to the disciples and found them sleeping for sorrow, [46] and he said to them, "Why do you sleep? Rise and pray that you may not enter into temptation."

No, the cup could not be removed from him. But Jesus knew enough, and had enough faith, to add that last clause to his prayer: "nevertheless not my will, but yours, be done."

Jesus also had the presence of mind to tell the disciples to pray for what they really needed. What they *wanted* was to keep Jesus safe from the authorities who wanted to kill him; what they *needed* was to be able to endure the next twenty-four hours without abandoning him.

Is God Listening?

Whenever we pray for healing, or to be spared some trouble, we should always remember how Jesus prayed: "Nevertheless not my will, but yours, be done." Whenever we're tempted to complain that God doesn't answer our prayers, we should remember Jesus' prayer in Gethsemane. Jesus did get an answer, but the answer was no. This was what had to be.

Paul had the same experience.

2 Cor 12:7-10

7 And to keep me from being too elated by the abundance of revelations, a thorn was given me in the flesh, a messenger of Satan, to harass me, to keep me from being too elated. 8 Three times I besought the Lord about this, that it should leave me; 9 but he said to me, "My grace is sufficient for you, for my power is made perfect in weakness." I will all the more gladly boast of my weaknesses, that the power of Christ may rest upon me.

10 For the sake of Christ, then, I am content with weaknesses, insults, hardships, persecutions, and calamities; for when I am weak, then I am strong.

Here again, Paul — the apostle who had faith enough to spread the Church throughout the northeastern Roman Empire, and on into Rome itself — prays for something specific, and the answer is no.

We don't really know what Paul's "thorn" was. It could have been anything — back trouble, gout, headaches, even a constant temptation that he had to work to overcome. Probably the Corinthians did know: they knew Paul personally, and might have heard him complain about it. He seems to write to them as if they knew what he was talking about.

Whatever it was, though, it bothered Paul enough that he begged the Lord three times to take it away. But it stayed with him.

It wasn't because of his lack of faith, Paul says: it was because God had a reason for that pain, whatever it was. Paul believes that this bodily pain, this constant reminder of his mortality, is what keeps him from getting "too elated." It keeps his pride in check.

After all, he had a lot to be proud of. Churches in nearly every major city of Asia and Greece looked to him as their founder. He could argue that he had accomplished more in spreading the Word than even Peter himself.

Paul spends a good bit of his second letter to the Corinthians rattling off his accomplishments — not out of pride, but because the Corinthians forced him into it. Some in Corinth disputed Paul's authority as an apostle; he needed to show them that Christ really had given him that authority.

"Not that we are competent of ourselves to claim anything as coming from us," he reminds them; "our competence is from God" (2 Cor 3:5).

So Paul recalls to their minds what they already should have known about him: all the trials he's endured, all the things he's accomplished. Paul had a lot to be proud of.

But that pride would have been fatal to his mission. The moment he began to give the credit to himself, and not to God, he would have lost the single-minded focus on Christ that made his missions possible.

> *Whenever we're tempted to complain that God doesn't answer our prayers, we should remember the experiences of Jesus and St. Paul.*

That, Paul says, is why he had this "thorn" — this constant reminder that he was weak on his own. When he prayed to have it taken away, the answer was no. Instead, the Lord told him, "My grace is sufficient for you, for my power is made perfect in weakness."

Grace Under Pressure

The great accomplishments weren't Paul's. They were Christ's.

The Lord gave Paul the power to do all these things, not just in spite of his weakness, but *because* of his weakness. That's why Paul's only "boast" is in his weakness:

2 Cor 4:7-11

[7] But we have this treasure in earthen vessels, to show that the transcendent power belongs to God and not to us. [8] We are afflicted in every way, but not crushed; perplexed, but not driven to despair; [9] persecuted, but not forsaken; struck down, but not destroyed; [10] always carrying in the body the death of Jesus, so that the life of Jesus may also be manifested in our bodies. [11] For while we live we are always being given up to death for Jesus' sake, so that the life of Jesus may be manifested in our mortal flesh.

Grace is divine *power*, not just undeserved favor. God doesn't just take pity on us, he empowers us — but only through our weakness and brokenness. Only when we cease to rely on our own strength can we discover that God's strength is always there for us.

People who think they stand had better take heed lest they fall. Our biggest problem is not our pain but our pride. Sometimes our pain helps us overcome our pride, and then that pain — even though it still hurts — is a good thing.

> *Because of the tender love our good Lord has for all those who shall be saved, he gives comfort readily and sweetly, assuring us, "It is true that sin is the cause of all this pain, but all shall be well, and all shall be well, and all manner of things shall be well."*
>
> — St. Julian of Norwich

St. Paul, in fact, even went so far as to celebrate his sufferings. He once wrote:

> We rejoice in our sufferings, knowing that suffering produces endurance, and endurance produces character, and character produces hope, and *hope does not disappoint us*, because God's love has been poured into our hearts through the Holy Spirit which has been given to us.
>
> — Rom 5:3-5 (EMPHASIS ADDED)

We should expect that our faith will be tested, like St. Paul's, and like Abraham's. But we know all the answers on that test. If we rely on our own strength, we fail. If we rely on God's strength, nothing can stop us.

That's because God doesn't just tell us to keep a stiff upper lip. God won't leave us trapped in bad times forever: he shows us the escape route.

How can we be sure? We have God's all-powerful guarantee, his promise. That is blessed assurance for those who have faith. Hope is, according to one classical definition, the certain expectation of future happiness. As St. Paul said, "I know whom I have believed, and I am sure that he is able to guard until that Day what has been entrusted to me" (2 Tim 1:12).

One of the smartest and holiest men who ever lived, St. Thomas Aquinas, felt confident enough to bet his life on it. He had every good reason, as we do, to live in certain hope, blessed assurance of salvation: "Hope does not trust chiefly in grace already received, but on God's omnipotence and mercy . . . Whoever has faith is certain of God's omnipotence and mercy."

Take Away

God's power is most evident in our moments of weakness.

CHAPTER 7

The Escape Route

Thou art my hiding place and my shield;
I hope in thy word.

— Ps 119:114

Though he trained his sights on glory, St. Paul knew that he would have to suffer much while he was "in the flesh" (Gal 2:20) and that he would die (Phil 1:23).

For those of us who don't share St. Paul's great theological gifts, suffering and death are profound mysteries. We know they entered the world because of sin (Rom 5:12). Yet we also believe that Christ has set us free from the power of sin and death (Rom 8:2).

If that's true, why must we still suffer loss and die?

Paul knew that Jesus Christ himself had suffered, not as a *substitute* for sinful humanity, but as our *representative*. Thus, Christ's saving passion didn't *exempt* us from suffering, but rather *endowed* our suffering with divine power and redemptive value.

St. Paul could even "rejoice" in his troubles, "knowing that suffering produces endurance, and endurance produces character, and character produces hope, and hope does not disappoint us, because God's love has been poured into our hearts through the Holy Spirit" (Rom 5:3-5).

> *Life himself came down to be slain; Bread came down to suffer hunger; the Way came down to endure weariness on his journey; the Fountain came down to experience thirst. Do you, then, refuse to work and to suffer?*
>
> — St. Augustine of Hippo

St. Paul gave us the key to suffering: "I consider that the sufferings of this present time are not worth comparing with the glory that is to be revealed to us" (Rom 8:18).

Through the Spirit of God, we are children of God — "sons in the Son," to use the classic phrase of the Church Fathers. And God gives his children everything he has, sharing even his divine nature (2 Pet 1:4). But he did not spare his Son from suffering. Suffering was central to Jesus' mission as redeemer. And so it is part of our share in his life and mission.

So suffering is not an optional component of Christian life. Remember what Paul told us: "We are children of God" and "fellow heirs with Christ, *provided we suffer with Him* in order that we may also be glorified with him" (Rom 8:16-17 [emphasis added]). No suffering, no glory.

But we can endure the suffering, because it's peanuts compared to the joy it's preparing us for. We can endure it because God is on our side.

The Only Real Escape

What we can't do is endure it on our own. We need help.

1 Cor 10:12-13

> [12] Therefore let any one who thinks that he stands take heed lest he fall. [13] No temptation has overtaken you that is not common to man. God is faithful, and he will not let you be tempted beyond your strength, but with the temptation will also provide the way of escape, that you may be able to endure it.

Now, this escape doesn't mean we can get out of the trial. No, our escape route leads right *through* the fire. That's why Paul says God "will also provide the way of escape, *that you may be able to endure it.*" Whatever is troubling us, we have to endure it. We have to suffer that temptation, that loss, that pain — and deal with it.

But God promises that we *can* deal with it — once we learn how weak and helpless we are.

We can't deal with it on our own. But if we're willing to lean on God — which often we can't really learn to do until all our other resources have been taken away from us — then God will pull us through the darkness and out the other side into the light. He'll give us the way of escape.

And that way is the sacraments.

The sacraments unify us with Christ. They make our own sufferings part of Christ's suffering.

Paul himself makes this connection. After he promises his readers "the way of escape," he immediately proceeds, in the very next verses, to map out the escape route for them. He urges them to shun the worship of idols for true worship — Eucharistic worship — and that is the way of escape!

"The cup of blessing which we bless, is it not a participation in the blood of Christ? The bread which we break, is it not a participation in the body of Christ?" (1 Cor 10:16). When we eat the bread and drink the wine, Christ's body and blood become our own. And we have the strength to endure the way Christ endured.

We endure our own trials, however great they may be, because we have the body that endured the worst trial of all time.

God is faithful, says St. Paul, and he will provide the way of escape.

I have been crucified with Christ; it is no longer I who live, but Christ who lives in me; and the life I now live in the flesh I live by faith in the Son of God, who loved me and gave himself for me.

— GAL 2:20

Here's where God's way and the world's way are strikingly different.

The world offers us a means of escape, too. Any number of means, in fact. And they all promise that we won't have to endure the suffering anymore.

Alcohol, sex, drugs — it's so easy to look to any of them as our escape route. They make the pain go away. They make us feel good again. At least for a short time.

> *Without the Holy Eucharist there would be no happiness in this world, and life would not be bearable.*
>
> — St. John Vianney

On the other hand, the Church only promises us that we'll have to go through the pain, but we'll have the strength to endure it.

That doesn't sound like much of a bargain.

And it wouldn't be if we didn't know now what hard times are for. Hard times bring us closer to God; they make us more like his Son. The substitute escapes the world offers us don't do that. They let us go merrily on our way to perdition, careening away from God, until nothing can bring us back.

Take Away

The sacraments provide our way of escape through troubles.

CHAPTER 8

The Touch of the Cross

WHENE'ER across this sinful flesh of mine
  I draw the Holy Sign,
All good thoughts stir within me, and renew
  Their slumbering strength divine;
Till there springs up a courage high and true
  To suffer and to do.

— VEN. JOHN HENRY NEWMAN,
"THE SIGN OF THE CROSS"

When Christ died on the Cross, he didn't take away our pain. He gave our pain and struggles a holy significance, a redemptive power, which makes it a privilege for us to suffer with Christ.

The Cross of Christ bestows a dignity even upon the small inconveniences of our lives. When we unite our troubles, great and small, with the suffering of Christ, we participate in the redemption of the world. We become fully human. We become heroes. We become godlike. We become all this because we become Christlike — though no one on earth may ever notice.

The effect of the Cross is like a Midas touch, raising infinitely the value of everything it blesses. Here is how a great Carmelite spiritual writer, Fr. Gabriel of St. Mary Magdalene, put it:

> Jesus calls our sufferings a *cross* because the word signifies the instrument of salvation; and He does not want our sorrows to be sterile, but to become a cross, that is, a means of elevating and sanctifying our souls. In fact, all suffering is transformed, changed into a cross as soon as we accept it from the hands of the Savior, and cling to His will which transforms it for our spiritual advantage. If this is true for great sufferings, it is equally true for the small ones; all are part of the divine plan, all, even the tiniest, have been predisposed by God from all eternity for our sanctification.

The effect of the Cross is like a Midas touch, raising infinitely the value of everything it blesses.

When hard times come, we begin our prayer with the Sign of the Cross, and we remember that God loves us. We bless our suffering with the holy sign, and we make it holy.

> *We must expect the cure of all our wounds from the Sign of the Cross.*
>
> — St. Maximus of Turin

We turn to the Church and the sacraments for the strength we need to endure. And we complain to God if we like — but we always keep up our faith.

God did not forsake David, even though things seemed pretty bad when he wrote Psalm 22. God did not forsake his own Son on the Cross, even though things were infinitely worse.

God will not forsake us, either.

The times are hard. But they're not worth considering when we compare them to the glory waiting for us.

We *will* endure. God *will* give us the strength.

And we can rejoice knowing that we suffer with Christ for a very short time, so that we can be with Christ in glory forever.

Take Away

Our sufferings have dignity because they are crosses, and they are Christ's.

An Act of Hope

O my God, relying on your almighty power and infinite mercy and promises, I hope to obtain pardon of my sins, the help of your grace and life everlasting, through the merits of Jesus Christ, my Lord and Redeemer. Amen.